STAR WARS
ADULT COLORING BOOKS

Vol.1

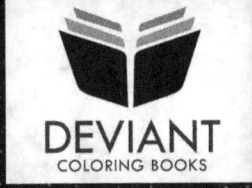

DEVIANT
COLORING BOOKS

INTRODUCTION

Star Wars is considered one of the greatest Science Fiction movies of all time. The film is about Palpatine's effort to gain control over galaxy and in order to do this he pitches the federation against the planet Naboo, resulting in a futuristic war in order to rule the galaxy. Star Wars made epic fantasy real and has defined cinema as pure visual and aural pleasure, mixed with basic emotional manipulation.

There are 6 parts of Star Wars: The Phantom Menace, Attack of the Clones, A New Hope, The Empire Strikes Back, Return of the Jedi and The Force Awakens. The original trilogy begins with the Galactic Empire nearing Death Star Space Station which will allow the empire to crush the rebels. Darth Vader captures princess Leia, an important member of the rebellion, who has stolen Death Star's blueprint and has it in a safe place.

Journey through this coloring book with droids, Hans Solo, Luke Skywalker, Obi Wan Kenobi, Finn, Rey and other heroes of the galaxy! Bring generations of space to life with a colored pencil, pen or crayon.

May the force be with you!

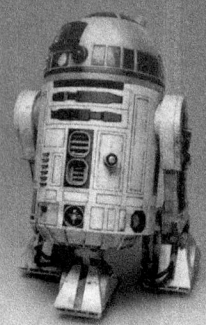

TABLE OF CONTENTS

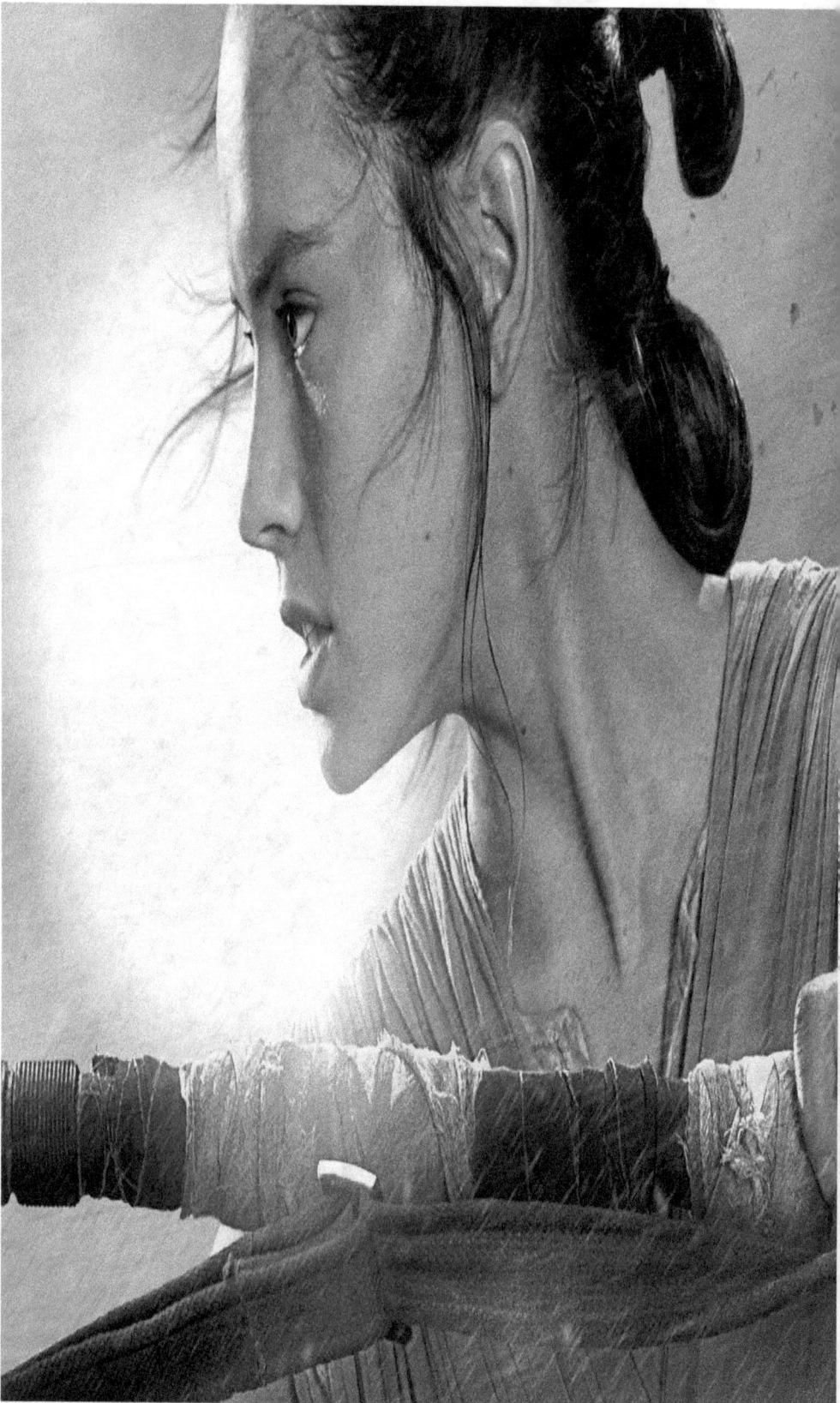

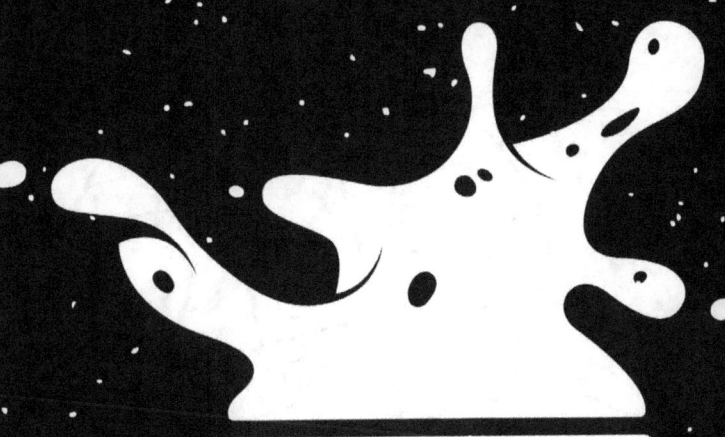

COME TO THE
DARK SIDE
OF THE
BEER

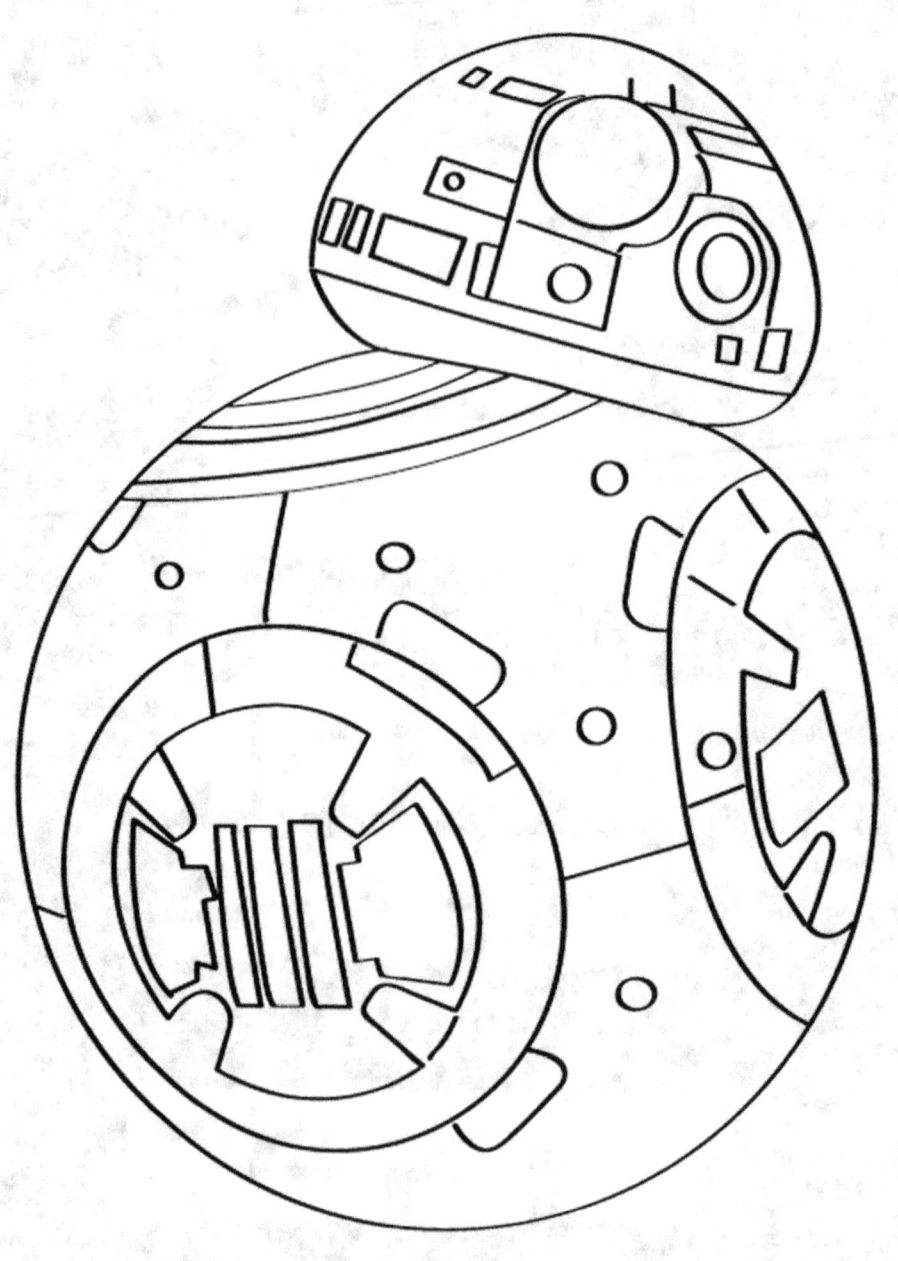

FIGURE 1: BB8

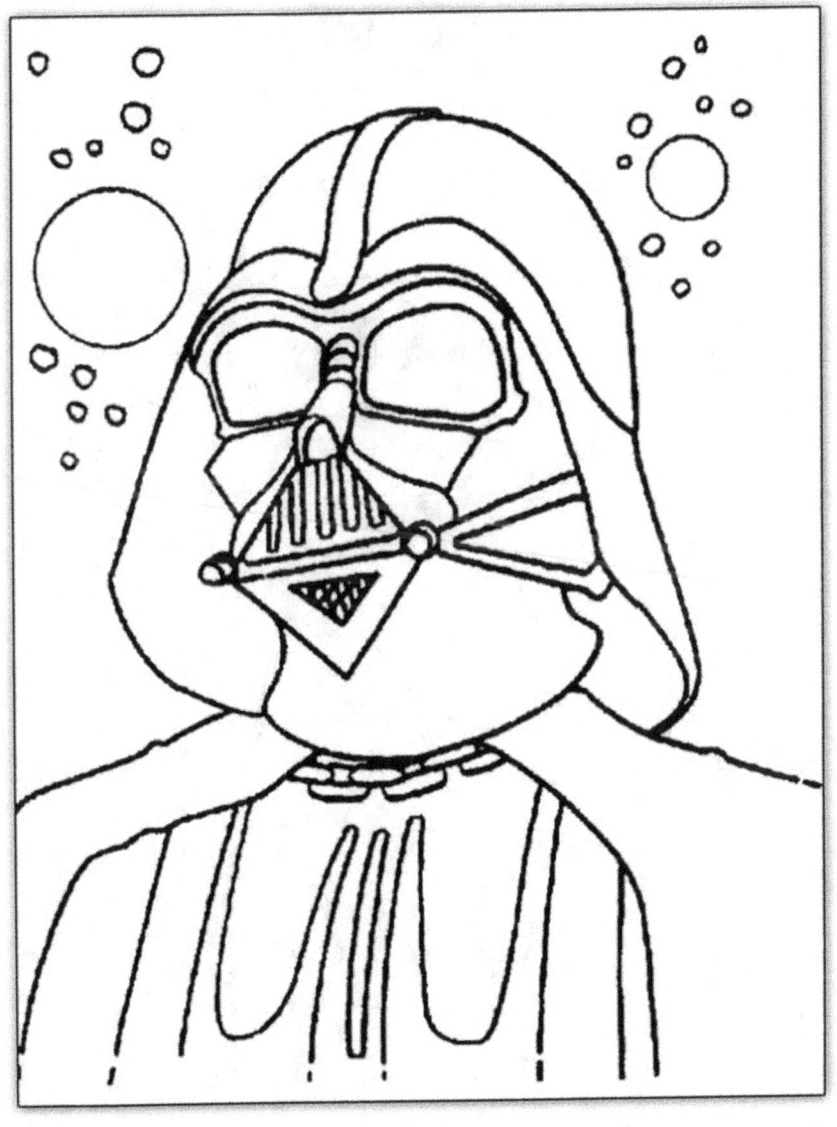

FIGURE 2: DARTH VADER

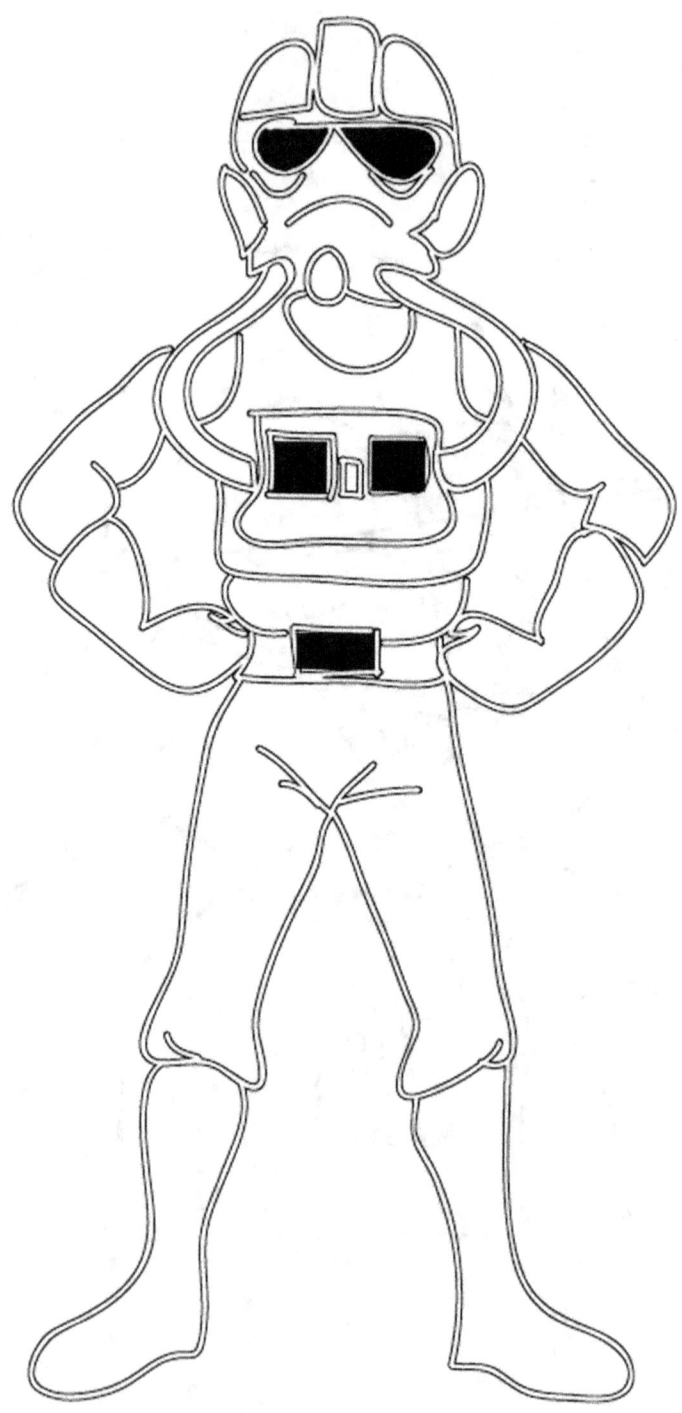

FIGURE 3: STORM TROOPER

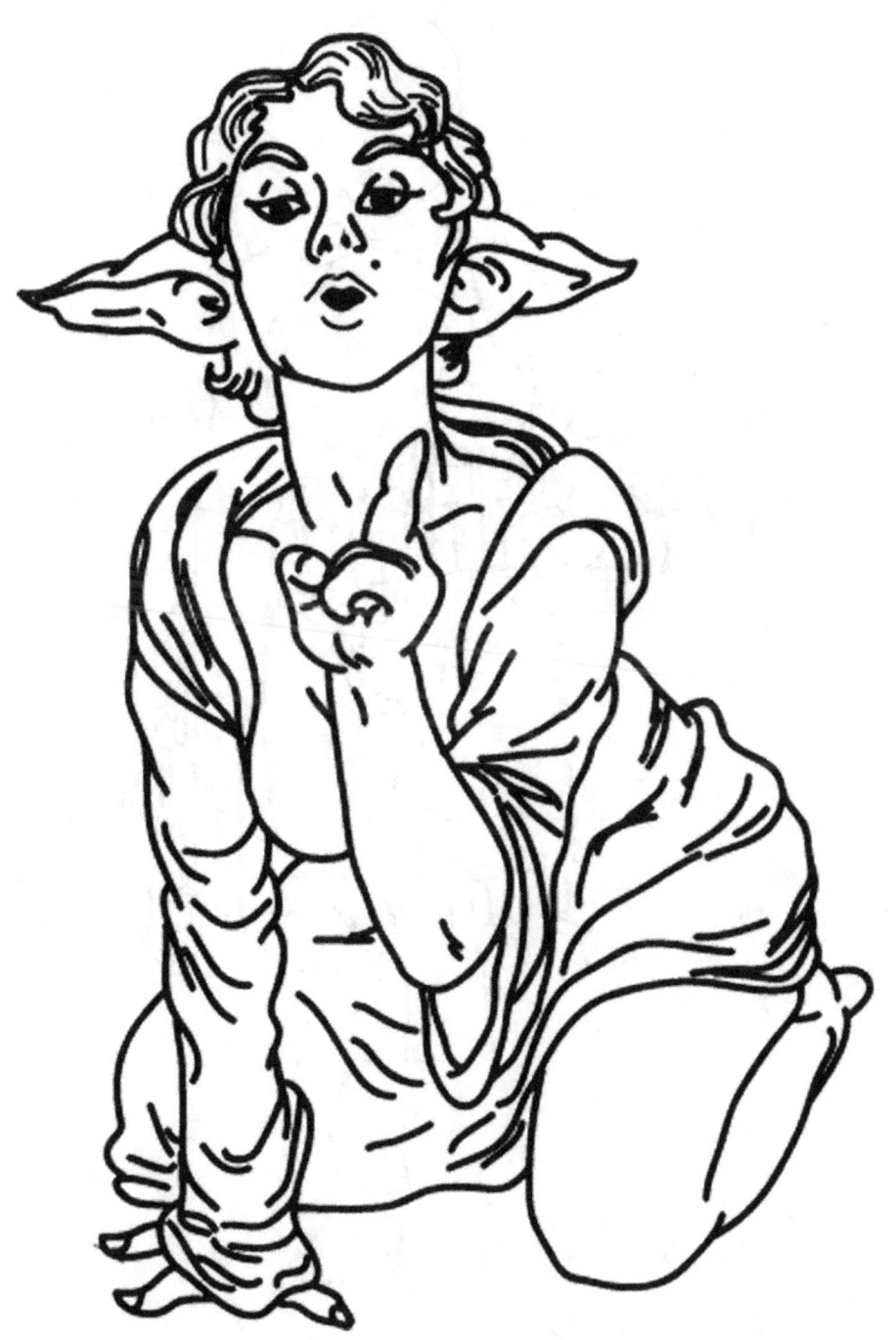

FIGURE 4: FEMALE YODA - YADDLE

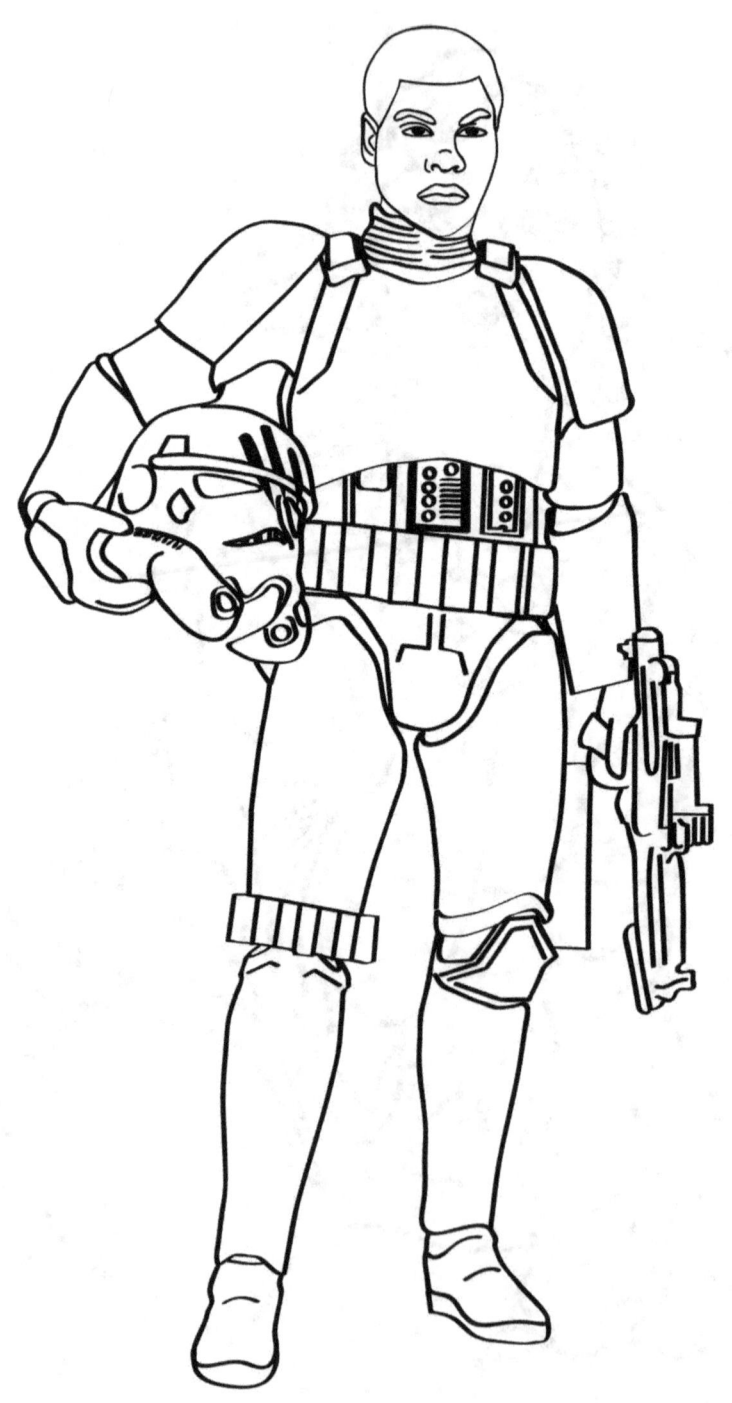

FIGURE 5: FINN

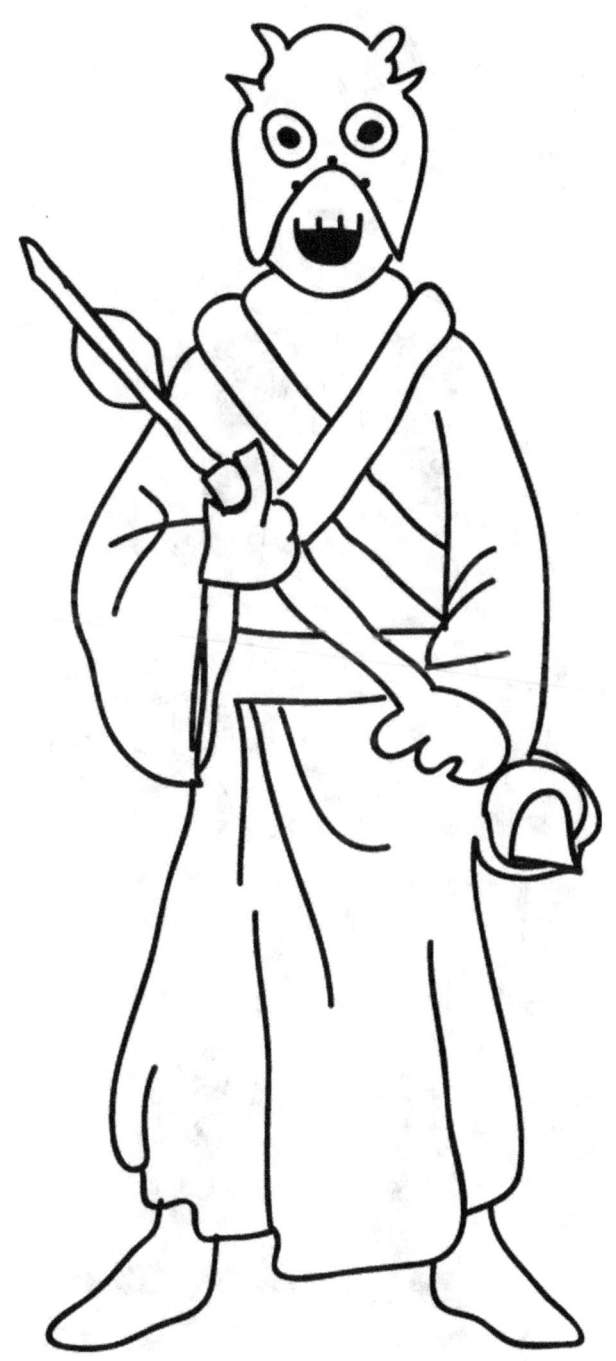

FIGURE 6: GREEDO

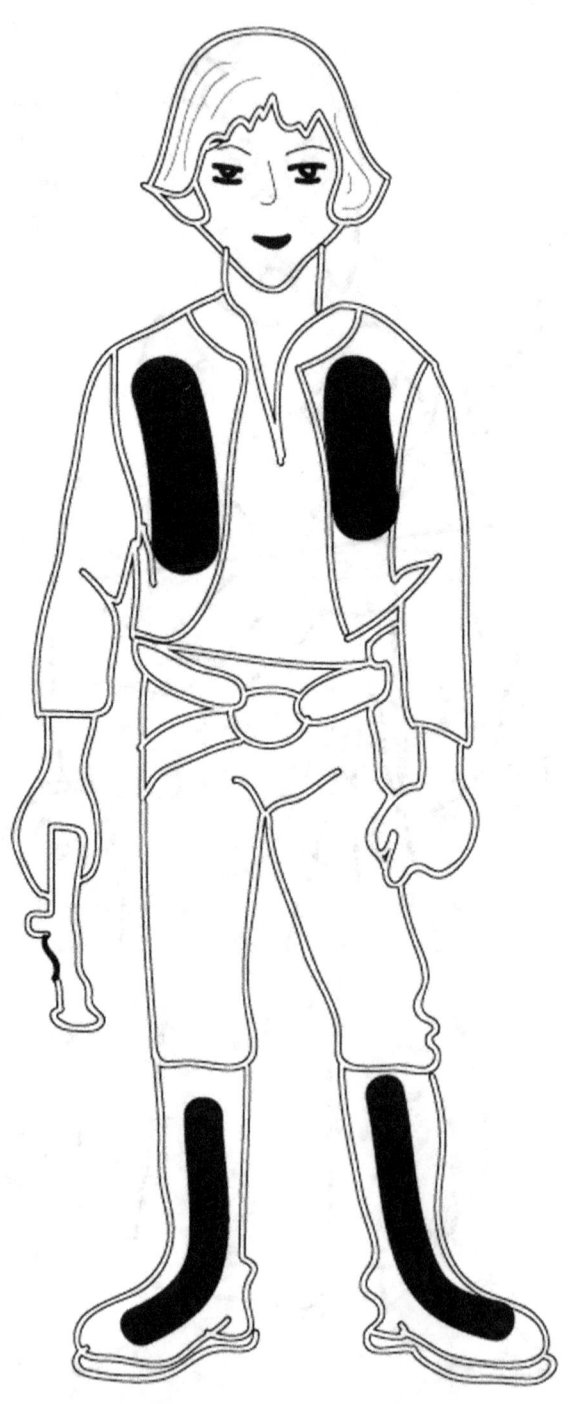

FIGURE 7: HANS SOLO

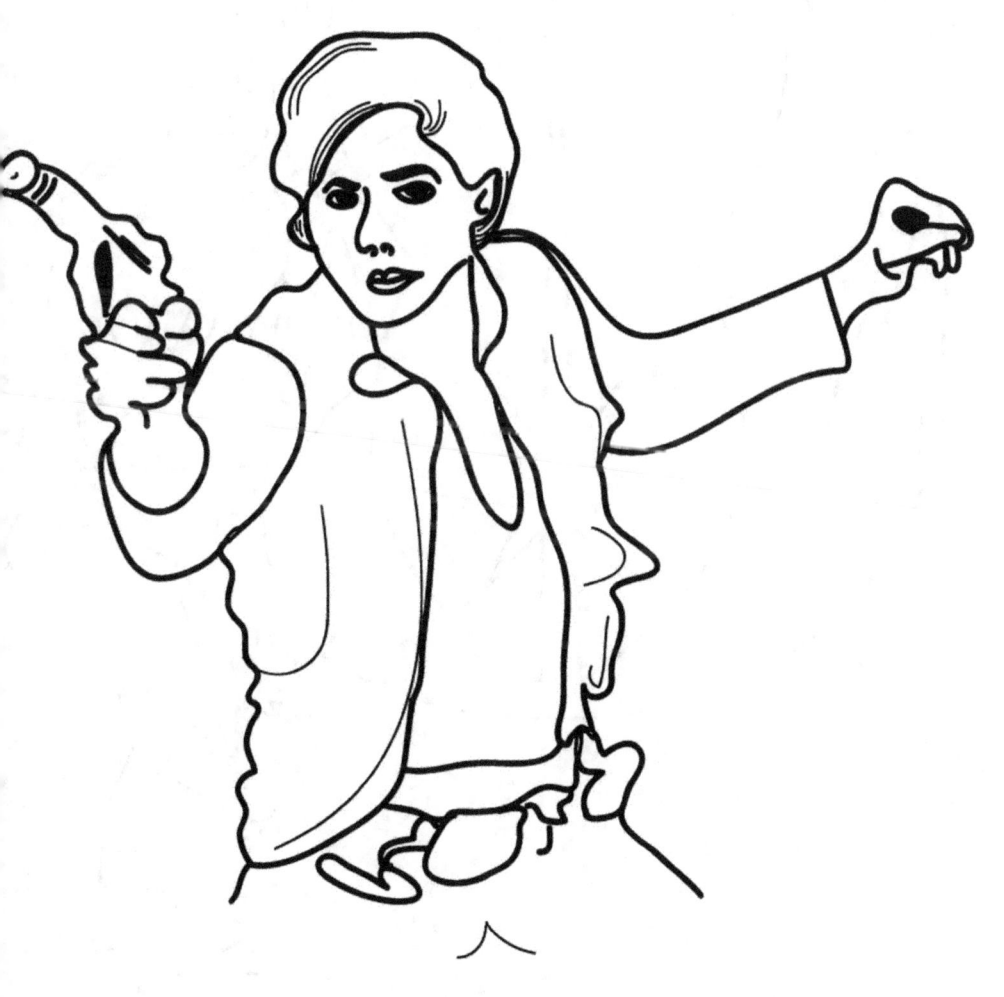

FIGURE 8: HANS SOLO

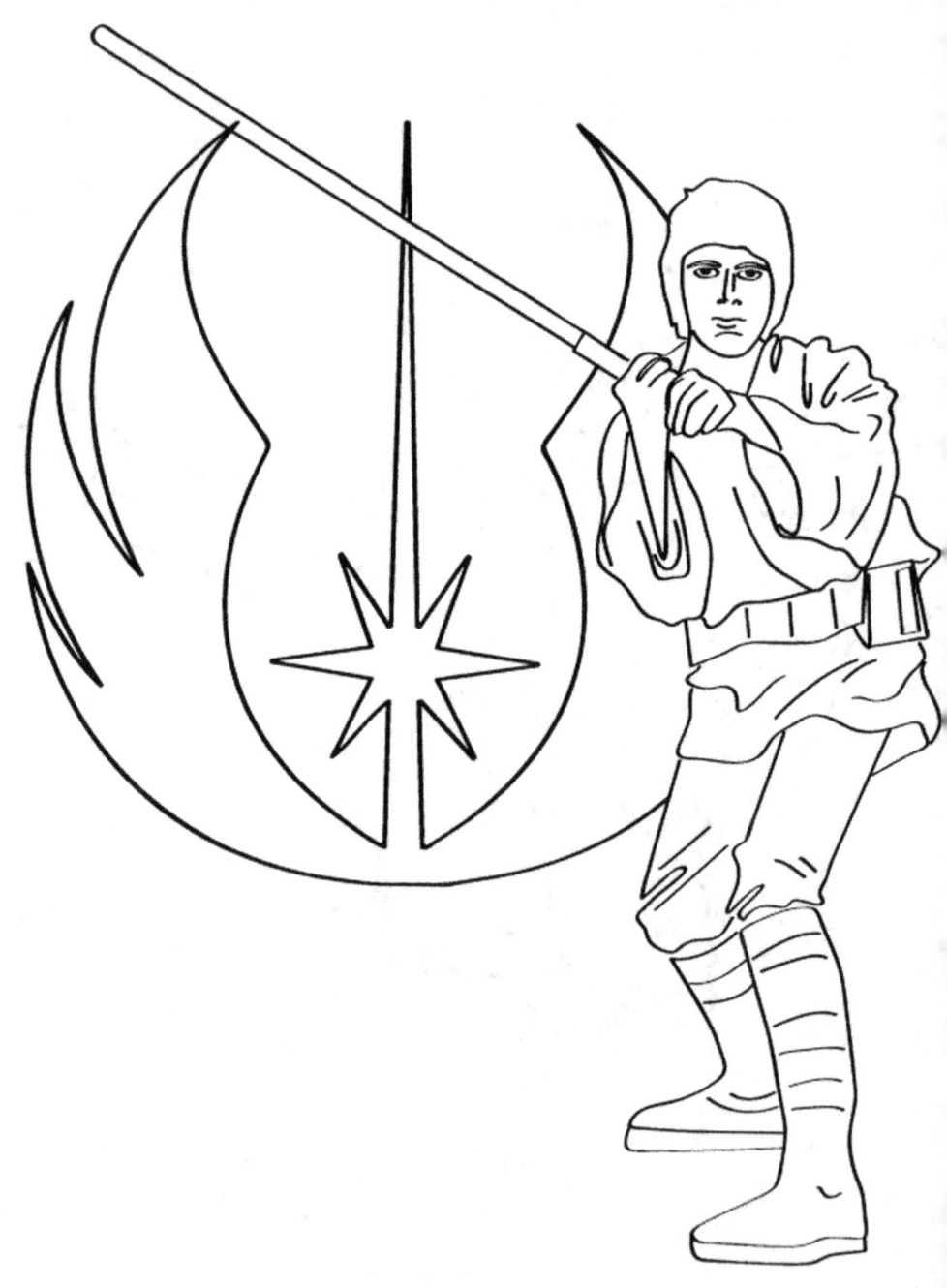

FIGURE 9: HANS SOLO

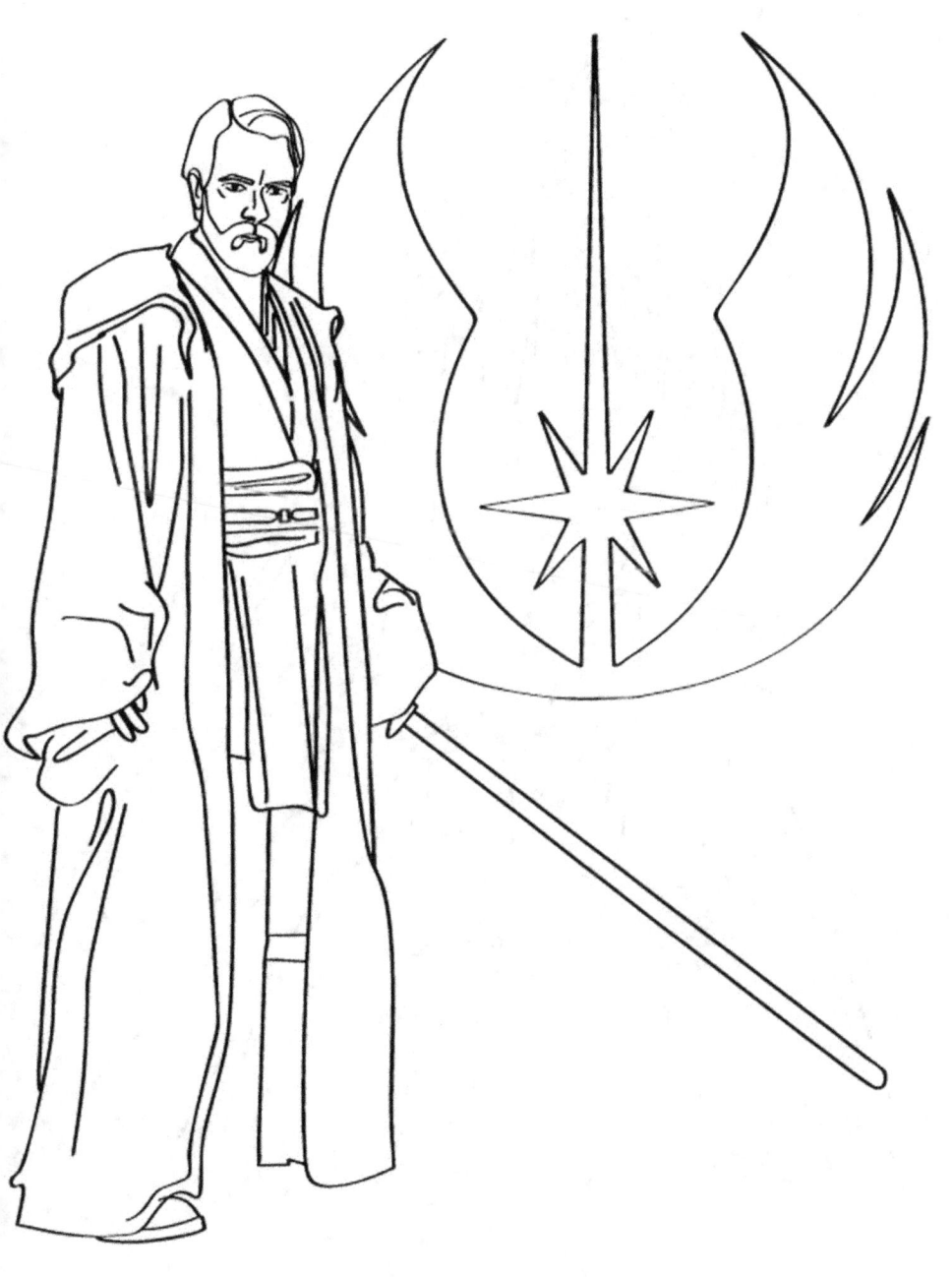

FIGURE 10: STAR WARS OBI WAN KENOBI

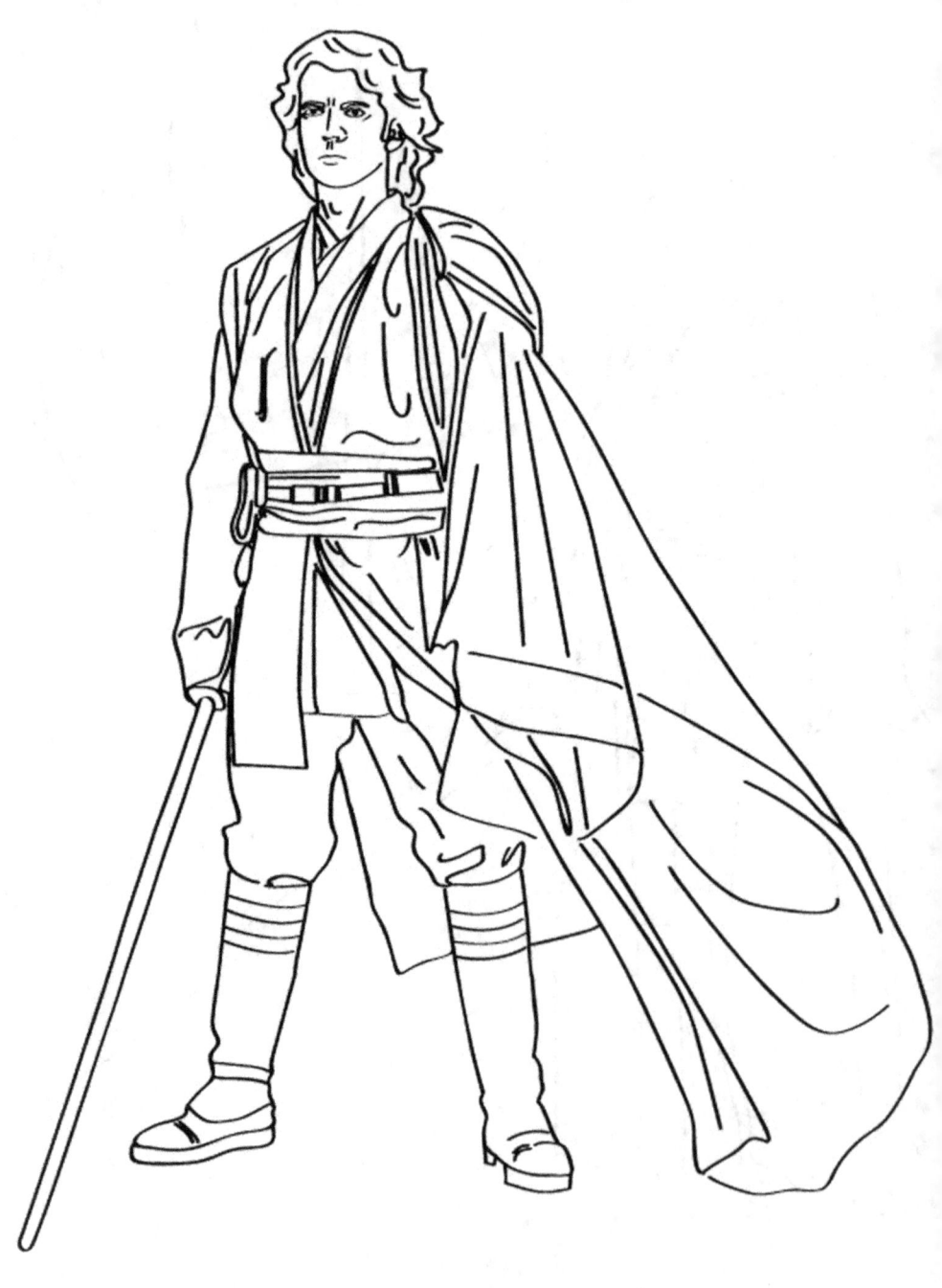

FIGURE 11: ANAKIN SKYWALKER

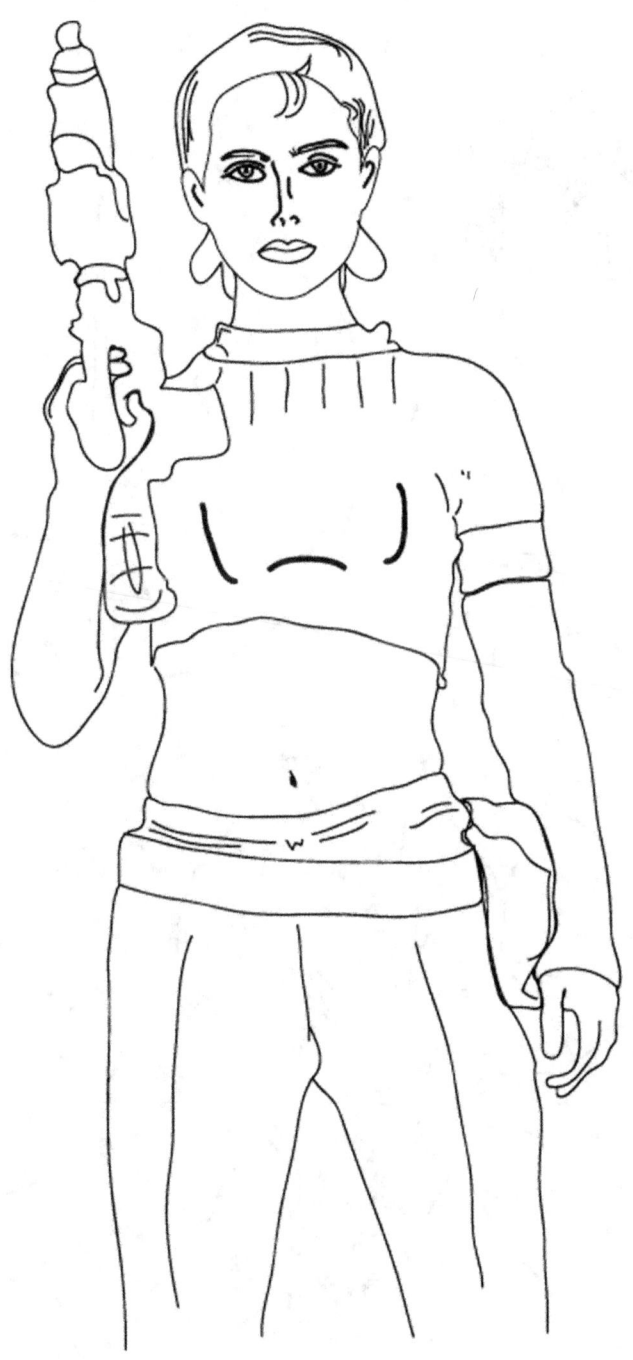

FIGURE 12: PADME AMIDALA

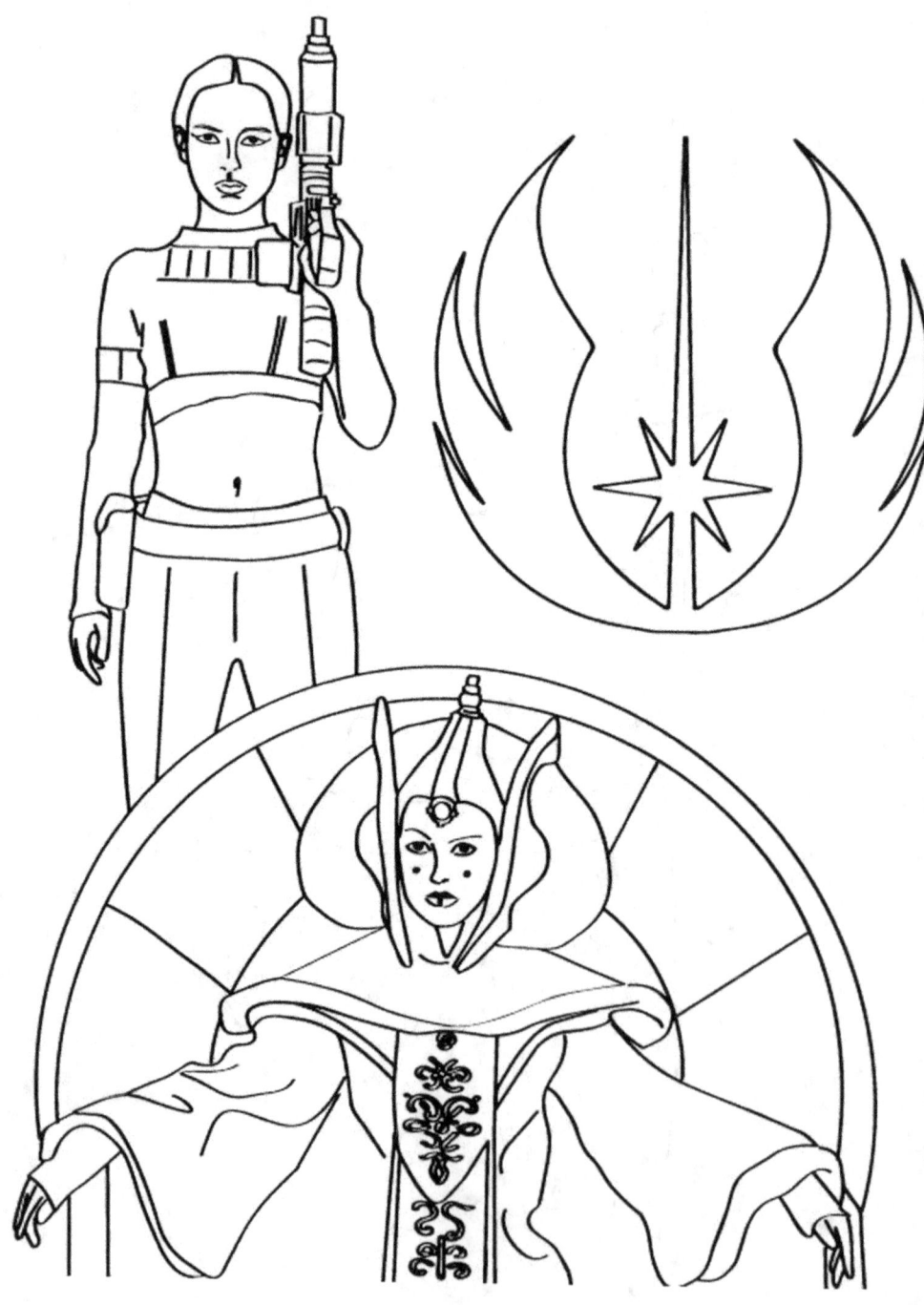

FIGURE 13: PRINCESS AMIDALA

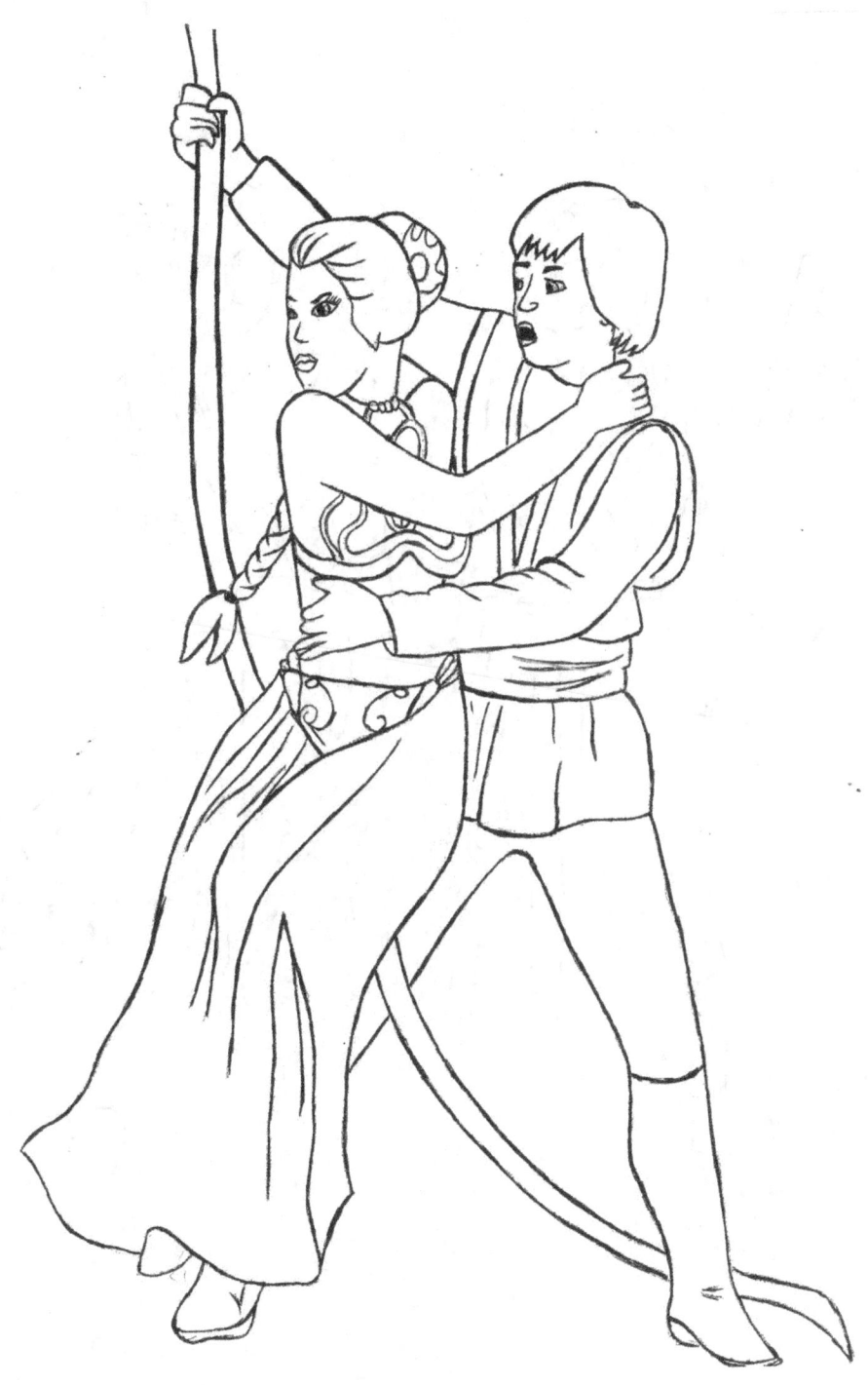

FIGURE 14: PRINCESS LEIA AND HAN SOLO

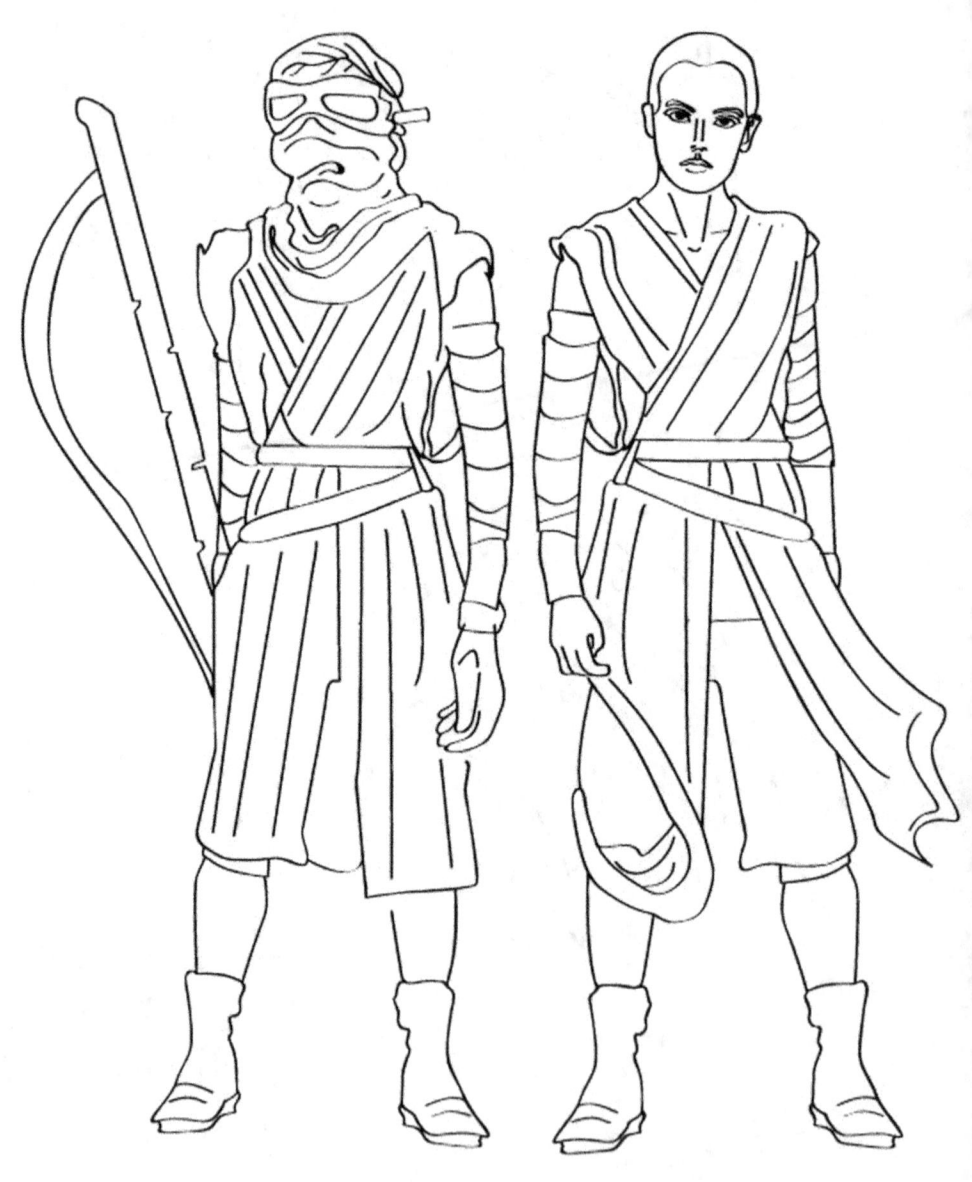

FIGURE 15: REY WITH AND WITHOUT MASK

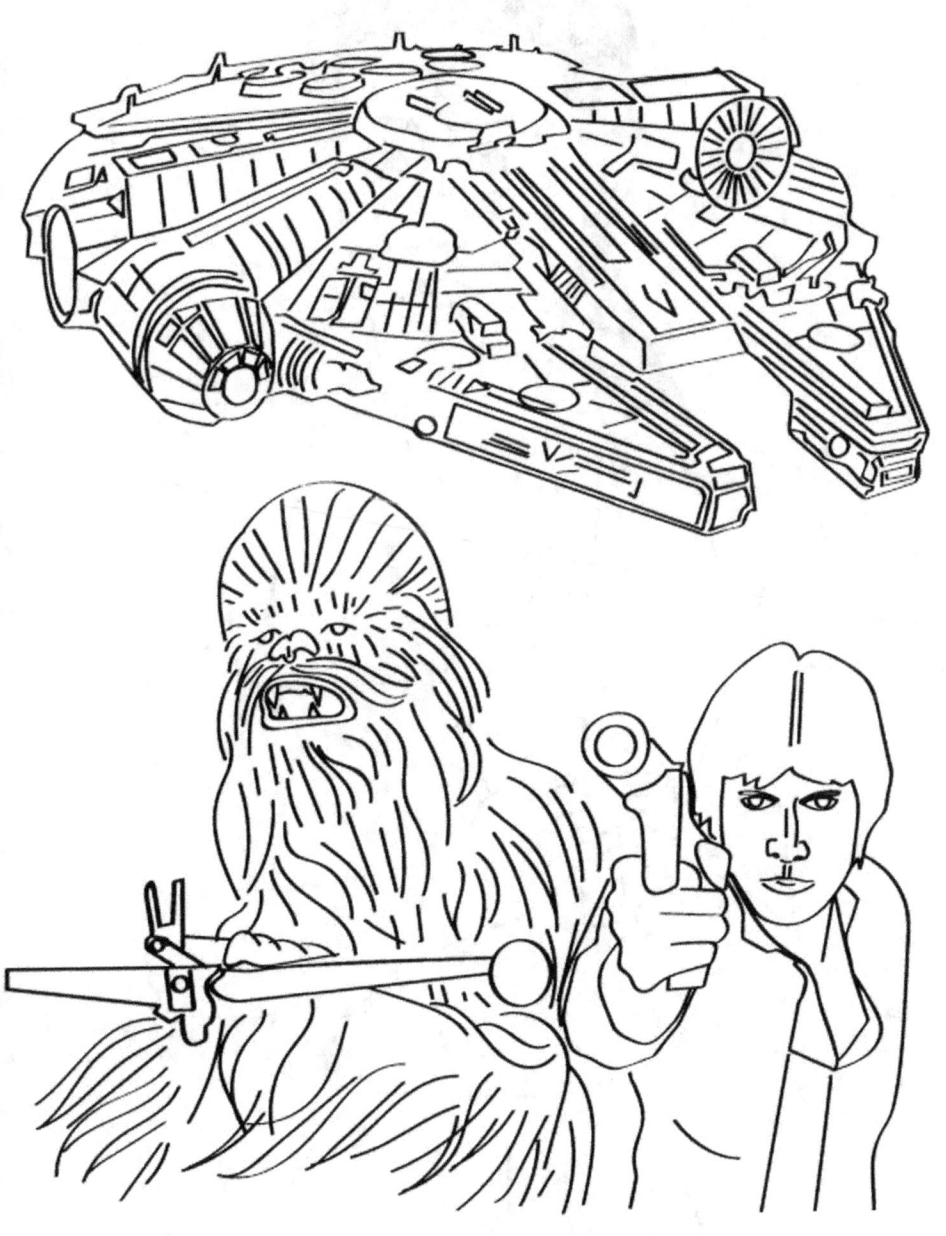

FIGURE 16: CHEWY AND HANS SOLO

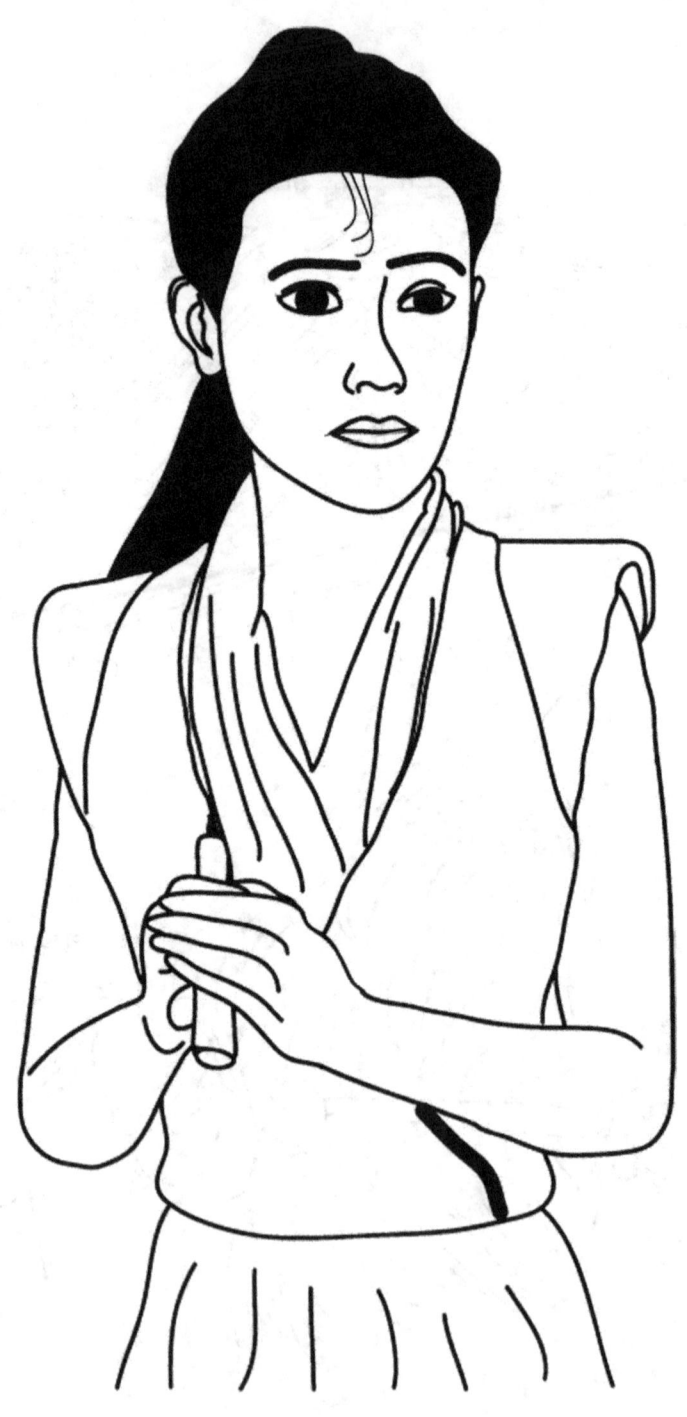

FIGURE 17: REY

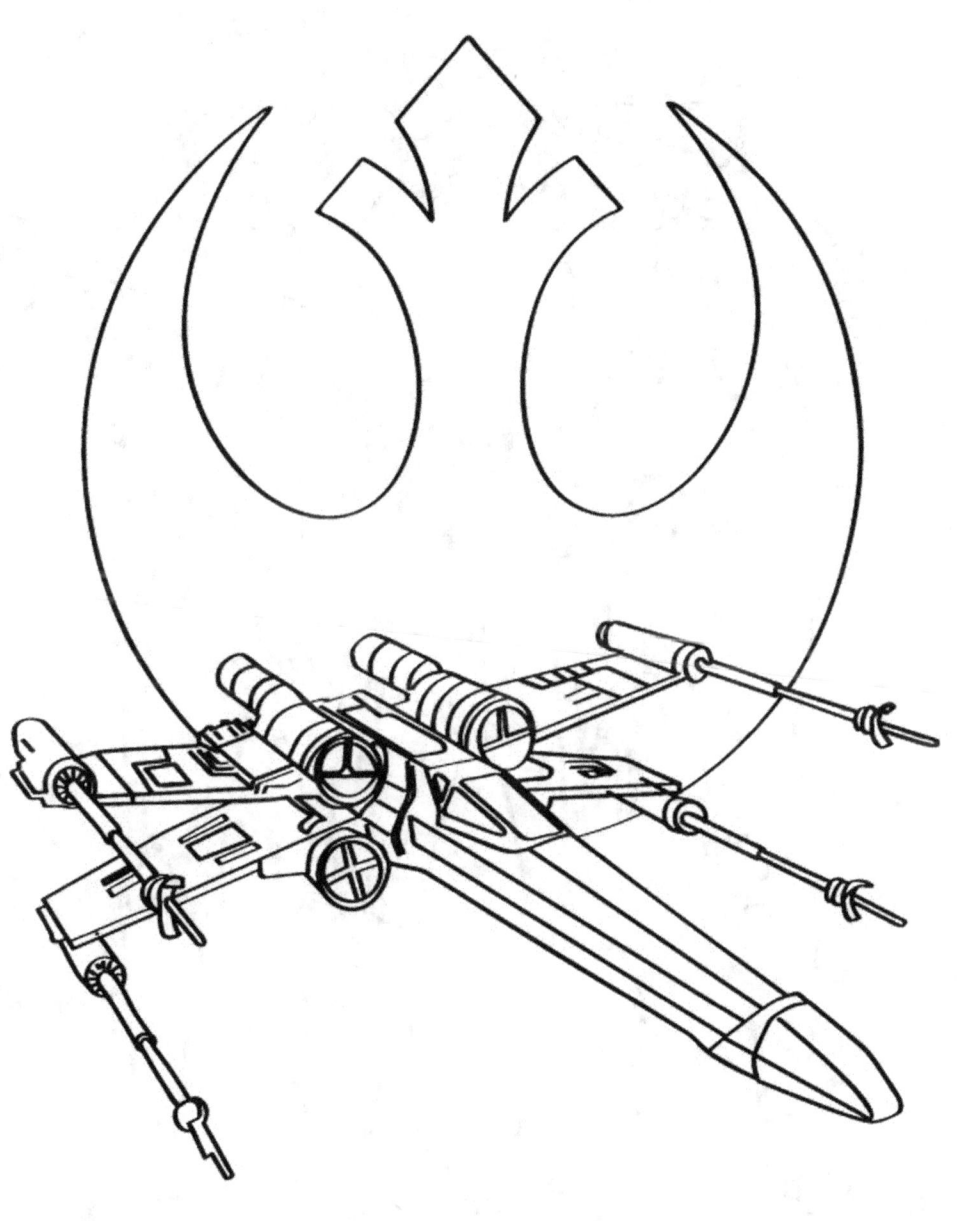

FIGURE 18: SPACESHIP OCCUPY

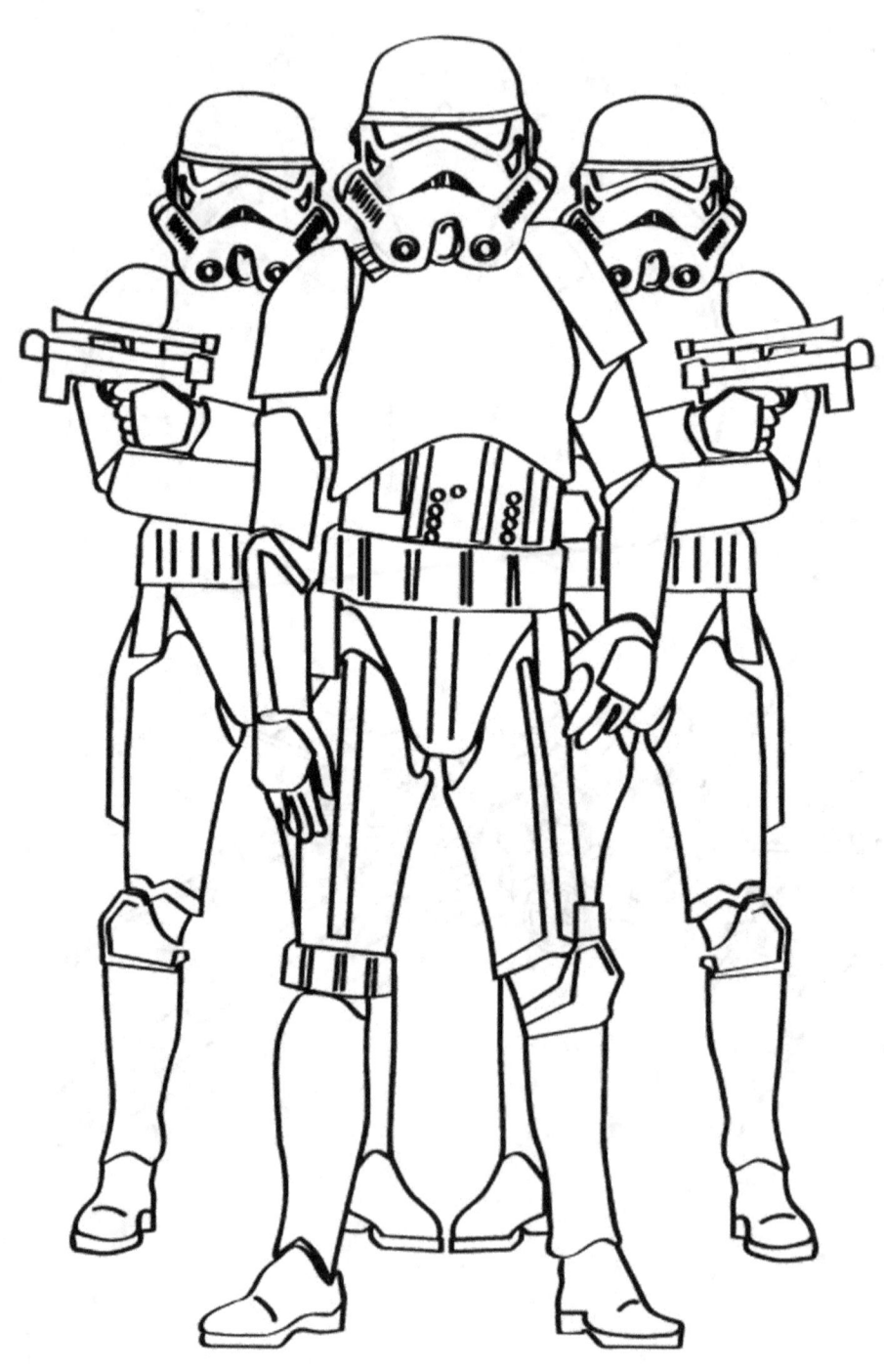

FIGURE 19: STORM TROOPERS

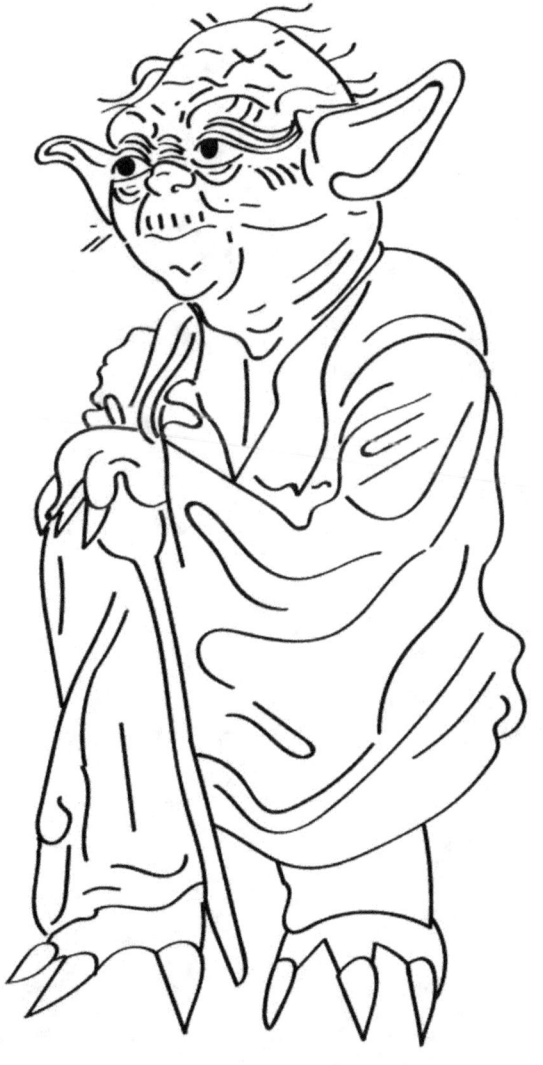

FIGURE 20: YODA